River
Friendly

River
Wild

Jane Kurtz

River Friendly River Wild

ILLUSTRATED BY

Neil Brennan

SIMON & SCHUSTER BOOKS FOR YOUNG READERS

For all my former neighbors
in the Lincoln Drive area,
one terrific neighborhood — J. K.

I'd like to thank Karen and Steve Harvey
for their cooperation, with a special thanks to Sarah Harvey
for being not just a great model, but a great kid! Thanks guys! — N. B.

SIMON & SCHUSTER BOOKS FOR YOUNG READERS

 An imprint of Simon & Schuster Children's Publishing Division
1230 Avenue of the Americas, New York, New York 10020

Text copyright © 2000 by Jane Kurtz
Illustrations copyright © 2000 by Neil Brennan
All rights reserved including the right of reproduction in whole or in part in any form.
SIMON & SCHUSTER BOOKS FOR YOUNG READERS is a trademark of Simon & Schuster.
Design by Heather Wood / The text for this book is set in Lomba Medium.
Printed in Hong Kong
1 3 5 7 9 10 8 6 4 2

Library of Congress Cataloging-in-Publication Data
Kurtz, Jane.
River friendly, river wild / by Jane Kurtz ; illustrated by Neil Brennan. — 1st ed.
p.   cm.
Summary : A family experiences a renewed appreciation for home and community
after they are evacuated during a spring flood and then return to survey the damage.
ISBN 0-689-82049-6
[1. Survival—Fiction. 2. Floods—Red River of the North—Fiction.
3. Grand Forks (N.D.)—Fiction.] I. Brennan, Neil, ill. II. Title.
PZ7.K9626Ri   2000   [E]-dc21   98-6945   CIP   AC

Artist's Note / *I use oil glaze. I start with a light sketch on a gessoed board, then I glaze over that with a thin layer of burnt sienna oil paint to create an underpainting. Over this I apply thin layers of color into different areas, such as the pink of a shirt or the blue-green of water. Then I cover the entire surface with a black glaze to create depth and shadow. The last step is to go back in with local color glazes to punch up the color and add highlights.*

Author's Note

On April 17, 1997—my birthday—air-raid sirens
sounded to let people know that Lincoln Drive, where
we had lived for about eight years, was in danger from
the rising Red River. Our house was on high ground.
But to be safe, we packed overnight bags and moved to
the house of some friends. On April 19 at 2:30 A.M., a
knock on the door let us know we had to evacuate from
that house. As the river continued to flow over the dikes,
one neighborhood after another was evacuated, until
almost every house in Grand Forks, North Dakota,
was empty.

    I wrote many of these poems in the weeks just
after the flood, while living in a borrowed house in
the small town of Walhalla. We moved from there to a
FEMA (Federal Emergency Management Agency) travel
trailer and then to a FEMA mobile home. Much of the
writing in these pages is drawn from our family's real
experience, but there are also bits and pieces of other
people's stories woven in. I offer the book in salute
to all of us who struggled through the 1997 flood and
years of recovery; to the volunteers from the Red Cross,
Salvation Army, and various churches who helped clean
up Grand Forks; and to anyone who has done the amazing
job of picking up life after a flood, tornado, hurricane,
fire, or other natural disaster.

The Red River

The river wiggled
like a fat brown thread
along the flat quilt of the Red River Valley,
stitching North Dakota and Minnesota together.
My friend Sarah and I
ran races up and down the dike.
In winter, we walked across the river
to touch Minnesota.
In spring, we sat on her back porch
and watched the river ripple.
Sometimes, full of spring rain,
it crawled up her yard,
leaving chunks of trees
that we made into pirate ships.
My brother, Max, fished on the river's banks.
Sometimes he let me carry his fishing pole
and I sat beside him,
loving the wet, muddy smell of the summer river.
One time, Max caught the biggest fish any of us ever saw.
I ran and got the scale.
We weighed it
and Max kissed it
and then he threw it back.
That was us.
That was the river.

Spring creeps into the city
one toe at a time.
Days are warm as the boots that snuggled my feet all winter.
Nights are cold.
"That's good," Mr. Ford from across the street says.
"Good because the ice won't melt too fast
and swell the river even more."
Snow piles that once were over my head
shrink until they're short as my waist.
Then the blizzard hits.
Ice slicks tree branches
and drips from telephone wires.
Electric poles fall down.
Power fizzles.
My dad makes a fire in the woodstove downstairs
and cooks hamburgers on top.
Max and I wiggle around in our sleeping bags
and play Monopoly.
Our cat, Kiwi, knocks the houses off with her paws.
We hardly miss the television at all.
As the snow starts falling, we drift asleep
deep in our bags,
close to the warm, black stove.

Snow's melting,

river's rising,

water's coming from the south

like a pickup truck in overdrive.

Everybody's bagging sand.

Piling the bags on top of the dikes.

One, lift, two, swing, three, catch, four, toss.

The water creeps into Sarah's yard.

The water creeps up to Sarah's back porch.

A truck rumbles by with sandbags for Sarah.

One, lift, two, swing, three, catch, four, toss.

A truck rumbles up to dump sand for Sarah.

Scrape, scritch, shovel the sand.

Swish, thump, drop it in the bag.

Wrist twist 'til the bag's closed.

Mom turns the wire to shut the bag's mouth.

One, lift, two, swing, three, catch, four, toss.

One, lift, two, swing, three, catch, four, toss.

River Wild

Melting snow has made the river wild.
Day after day,
it pushes the dikes,
where people walk, two by two,
looking for cracks that could sprout
and let river trickle through.
"Don't worry," Dad says.
"We're on high ground for Lincoln Drive.
I don't think the water could possibly get up here."
But I go off to school worrying anyway.

By noon, the classrooms buzz with stories of cracks.
"Don't worry," Mom says when I come home for lunch.
"Engineers are working on the dike."
I walk back to school, watching
our neighbors sandbag
relentlessly.
I'm at the swings when air-raid sirens
rise and fall and swell the air.
Parents pop up from everywhere.
Sarah and I hold hands
and stare at each other.
"Call me," she says,
as her mom runs up.
I call all afternoon,
but she never answers.

Just in Case

At supper,
everyone is as quiet
as unturned pages in a book.
"Let's pack one bag," Mom says finally.
"Just one bag.
Just in case."
"Can I pack the cat?" I ask.
"If we *do* leave," Dad says,
"it will only be for a couple days.
She'd be much happier at home."
I pack
four books
three shirts
two pairs of jeans.
Then I lie in bed,
while my heart pumps
like a rowing machine.
Dad tucks me in.
"Promise me one thing, okay?" I say.
"Put out lots and lots and lots and lots
of food and water for Kiwi.
Just
in
case."

Fleeing—Just After Midnight—April 18

Most things you lie awake and worry about
don't happen.
This
one
does.
Sirens *woooo wooo* wake us up.
Woooo, wooooo.
Everybody out.
I cry over Kiwi.
Max kisses Kiwi.
We grab our bags.
Rush, rush, everybody out.
I blow kisses to Kiwi.
Max cries over Kiwi.
We rush—
hush—
through the midnight streets
out of the silent city
away from the river
away from our home.

The Night the Buildings Burn—April 19

The shelter cots are hard and squeaky
when people turn at night.
I can stretch and touch
Mom and Dad and Max
but I miss that motor-stomach Kiwi cat.
Suddenly, everyone's up and staring.
"Look at the television," someone says.
Black, thick smudge of smoke.
What's happening? What's wrong?
How can things burn
when they're sitting in water?
Fire tongues lick the sky.

Is the world burning up? I'm scared.
Will the buildings all catch fire? I'm scared.
Will the downtown all catch fire? I'm too scared to go to sleep.
Will the homes all catch fire? On TV the walls fall down
"I don't know," Dad says. again and
"I don't think so," Mom says. again and
The sky turns red. again and
The sky turns black. again.

Ocean of Feelings

Two weeks of waiting
to find out if we have anything left.
My parents don't know what to do.
They wander around like balls of string,
winding and unwinding.
My mom makes lists
of everything she might have lost.
I wonder where Sarah is
and if Kiwi is scared
in our island house
with a rush of water all around.
On TV, we watch our city
where people navigate the river-streets
in any way they can.
They wade.
They rumble in Humvees.
They ripple through the streets in boats,
ducking under power lines.

"That used to be Lincoln Drive," a reporter says.
"Now it's Lincoln Lake."
"Look." Max points. "It's Sarah's house."
All I see is a roof.
I go out and sit on the porch.
Mom comes out with a squeezy hug.
"Want to try on the nice dress Grandma sent?"
"It's not my dress."
"Want to go find the library?"
"I'm never reading a book again
because I can't have my own books."
"We *do* have a nice house to stay in," she says.
"Wasn't it nice we could borrow this house?"
It was nice, but I want to go home.
Mom and I cry with our arms around each other.
"Come on," I finally tell her.
"I'll help you find the library."

All winter, cars leaped
from behind giant snowbanks,
making brakes slam,
making hearts thud.
When they finally let us back in the city,
the snow is gone, but
snowbanks of garbage
and sandbags
line every street,
making brakes slam,
making hearts hollow.
Mattresses,
lamps,
rocking horses,
and sleds,
furnaces,
water heaters,
doors and doors.
Every pile is someone's story.
Every story is sad.

Danger

The newspaper says:
Beware the river water.
It's contaminated with chemicals.
And be careful going back into your house.
The steps could be crumbled.
The floors could be buckled.
The stairs could be slick.
The windows could be broken,
and snakes could be inside.

We creep
up the steps
through the door.
"Kiwi?" I call.
No answer.
"Kitty, kitty," I call.
No cat.
I rumble around the two upstairs bedrooms
like a car that's lost its steering.
I creep down the slimy stairs.
My dad lifts a box and turns it over.
Water and paper dolls gush out.
The paper dolls
saw it all.
I wish they could tell me what happened to my cat.

Camping in the House

No cooking.
No warm water.
No heat.
We flip switches
by habit.
No lights go on.
At night, silence settles,
pumps stop humming outside.
We go to bed early
as the sun drops down.

My toes wince on the icy floor
and I wish for the wood-burning stove.
But it's downstairs
with curls of mud
and orange rust.
We wiggle
deep in our bags
around the glow
of an oil lamp.
I can't believe it's even our house.

Cleanup—May 5

My feet shiver in the big gray boots.
My hands shiver in the yellow rubber gloves.
I can see my breath
in what used to be my closet.
I don't love the smell of the river water
anymore.
In the dark downstairs,
I stumble on a lump.
"Don't step on the carpet with your muddy boots,"
Mom hollers.
She and I both giggle.
The carpet feels like an elephant
as we work to drag it out.
Max stands by a puddle in his room.
"Eeek!" he shrieks.
We all jump.
"False alarm," he says. "Fake snake."

The Red Cross truck *beep beeps* by with lunch.
"Thank you," my dad says.
"You're welcome," the Red Cross person says.
"You'd do the same for us."
People I never met made this lunch for me.
People I never met sent a planeload full of stuff.
Kids I never met made pictures of my school.
Someday, I'll do the same for someone else.
And when I see Sarah again,
I'm giving her the money Grandma sent for new dolls.
Some of my dolls were safe upstairs,
but Sarah's dolls must all be gone.

The Christmas Box

Red and silver garland
spills onto the ground.
Wet, red paint
from ornaments I made last year
streaks the cardboard box.
We reach inside
with yellow gloves
and cradle handfuls out.
The stockings Aunt Emily cut and sewed
the year that I was born.
The bird that sat in our Christmas tree
to bring us new year's luck.
The wreath Max made with five-year-old handprints
and lots of bright-green paint.
"It's hard to throw out memories," Mom says.
Her eyes are fat with tears.
Blue mold speckles a wooden box
that my great-grandpa carved.
Everything falls
in the black plastic bag
that will go to the curb
with everything else.
"Look," Mom says.
"Three glass angels.
I can clean these.
They're survivors of the flood—
like us."

The Most Terrible Part

Down beside the dike,
it's terrible.
A van went through a person's wall.
A hockey net hangs from a tree.
A house that floated
landed later
in someone else's yard.
I walk home slowly, in the rain,
looking up at Lincoln School.
The windows look back
like empty eyes.
Two blocks away,
a square machine
with a wide, wide mouth
scooches crablike down the street
to pick up freezers and stoves.

A block away,
a big machine
with a *looong* neck
lumbers and swings,
nudges
a pile of garbage into the street
and picks it up in its teeth.
The machines have names like
Komatsu and Case,
Cat and Deere.
They call to each other
in high yellow beeps.

Sarah's mom is outside their house
wearing a garbage bag over her clothes,
wearing a white mask over her face.
"Where's Sarah?" I ask.
"At her grandma's," she says.
"I'll tell her to call you.
She misses me.
She misses you.
She wants to come home.
But this isn't home.
Is it?"

I'm mad at the flood
because my cat is gone and
because Sarah's living at her grandma's now.
I'm mad at this doll
because she was upstairs, so she's fine
and my favorite doll wasn't, so she isn't.
I'm mad at these books
because they used to look like books
and now they're
gooshy
soggy
slimy
lumps
that no one will ever want to read.
I'm mad at all the piles of garbage
clogging up the sidewalks.
I wish the machine with the mouth
would get to our block
and gobble all this garbage up.
I'm mad at my mom
because she makes me eat the Red Cross hot meal
before I eat the Red Cross snacks.
"We're lucky to have something hot to eat," she says.
I know she's right.
But I don't feel lucky.

The New Dike

The city's cleaning up.
Kids wearing orange streamers on their arms
pick plastic bags
like flowers
from the bushes where the river left them.
A row of stuffed animals
sits on a couch
on the curb,
waiting to be picked up.
People are planting flowers.
But in our neighborhood,
they say a new dike
will barrel through the middle,
sweeping away my house,
sweeping away Sarah's house,
sweeping the school and other homes away.

Mr. Ford sits by the curb on his couch
and talks to everyone who walks by.
He's lived here all his life.
Now he's getting ready to move.
He shows me a table he got from his mom.
"It's been through four floods," he says.
"This one finally got it."

Mom and Dad rest,
as dirty as smudge pots.
"We'll be telling stories of this flood
for a long, long time," Dad says.
A squirrel runs by the ash tree
that Max planted in fourth grade.
It's popping with buds.
The flood didn't get the tree,
but the new dike will.

One Terrific Neighborhood—May 20

"This was a great neighborhood," Dad says.
"Old-fashioned," Mom says.
"You could borrow a cup of sugar
from anyone."
"Our next-door neighbor always brought in
our mail when we were gone," Max says.
"And fed Kiwi," I say.
We sit, trying to look at Mr. Ford's tulips
instead of the garbage piles.
The lawn is strewn with violets
and Mom's drying papers.

And then,
on careful feet,
around each paper
steps
a Kiwi cat.

I scream and run to pick her up.
Her tail tickles my neck.
Our next-door neighbor hurries over.
"Just got back to town," he says.
"The day after we all left,
I came in with my waders
to check on the pump.
Saw your cat
looking out the window.
Well, we still had your key."
"Where are you staying?" Dad asks.
"Heading out," he says.
"The store is gone.
Time to start over—someplace else."
Kiwi rumbles on my lap.
"You know," Dad says,
"this was one terrific neighborhood."

Memories

The river is back in its banks again
and here we are,
alive.
I know now that
some memories live in things—
in old clothes and photographs,
drawings and trees.
Some of those memories we'll have to let go.
But Mom and Dad and Max and Kiwi
and Sarah and I
will make new memories
and hold tight to the old ones that stick.
And then there's next Christmas,
when Mom says
for sure
the three flood angels
will shimmer
and glimmer
and shine
again
on our Christmas tree,
wherever
in the whole world
we are.